Property Investing:

How to Create Wealth and Passive Income Through Smart Buy & Hold Real Estate Investing. An Exact 18-Month Strategy for Making an Extra 100k Per Year

© **Copyright 2017 by _____ - All rights reserved.**

The follow eBook is reproduced below with the goal of providing information that is as accurate and reliable as possible. Regardless, purchasing this eBook can be seen as consent to the fact that both the publisher and the author of this book are in no way experts on the topics discussed within and that any recommendations or suggestions that are made herein are for entertainment purposes only. Professionals should be consulted as needed prior to undertaking any of the action endorsed herein.

This declaration is deemed fair and valid by both the American Bar Association and the Committee of Publishers Association and is legally binding throughout the United States.

Furthermore, the transmission, duplication or reproduction of any of the following work including specific information will be considered an illegal act irrespective of if it is done electronically or in print. This extends to creating a secondary or tertiary copy of the work or a recorded copy and is only allowed with express written consent from the Publisher. All additional right reserved.

The information in the following pages is broadly considered to be a truthful and accurate account of facts and as such any inattention, use or misuse of the information in question by the reader will render any resulting actions solely under their purview. There are no scenarios in which the publisher or the original author of this work can be in any fashion deemed liable for any hardship or damages that may befall them after undertaking information described herein.

Additionally, the information in the following pages is intended only for informational purposes and should thus be thought of as universal. As befitting its nature, it is presented without assurance regarding its prolonged validity or interim quality. Trademarks that are mentioned are done without written consent and can in no way be considered an endorsement from the trademark holder.

Table of Contents

Introduction 1
Chapter 1: Property Investment Mindset 3
Chapter 2: Finding the Money 7
Chapter 3: Mistakes to Avoid 15
Chapter 4: Getting Started with Your 18-month Strategy 21
Chapter 5: Flipping Properties 27
Chapter 6: Rental Properties 34
Conclusion 43
Description 44

Introduction

Congratulations on downloading *Property Investing: How to Create Wealth and Passive Income Through Smart Buy & Hold Real Estate Investing. An Exact 18-Month Strategy for Making an Extra 100k Per Year* and thank you for doing so. Real estate investment is one of the oldest and most reliable forms of investment in the world and if you follow the plan outlined in the following chapters you can start seeing real results in just a year and a half.

This doesn't mean that doing so will be easy, however which is why the following chapters will discuss everything you need to do in order to get into the real estate game successfully and also see real results from doing so. First you will learn about the true real estate investor mindset. Then you will learn about the ways you can find money to fund your real estate investment dreams without having to pony up the full cost yourself. From there you will learn about real estate investment mistakes to avoid on your journey to financial freedom. Next you will learn what you need to get started on your 18-month journey before finally learning how to go about making a profit from flipping houses and then using those profits to ultimately generate long-term income through investing in rental properties.

There are plenty of books on this subject on the market, thanks again for choosing this one! Every effort was made to ensure it is full of as much useful information as possible, please enjoy!

Chapter 1: Property Investment Mindset

In order to invest in real estate successfully, especially if you hope to make $100,000 in the next 18 months, you need to have a mindset that is primed for success. That means you need to cultivate the following suggestions into your daily life. Don't try to incorporate them, make a concentrated effort to do whatever needs to be done to ensure you build your investment mindset in the right way, starting right now.

Have the right perspective: First things first, it is important to develop a long-term perspective when it comes to investing in real estate successfully. Sure, if you follow the plan outlined in this book, you stand a good chance of making $100,000 in the first 18 months, but you are also going to want to look beyond this timeline if you hope to truly be successful in the real estate investment industry. Likewise, it is important to keep in mind that something is likely going to come along and shake up your plan every few months. The way you deal with these upsets is going to go a long way to determining what kind of real estate investor you really are. Don't let them shake your commitment, remain committed to the cause and will yourself to find the success you seek.

Be disciplined: In order to reach your initial goal in just 18 months, you are going to need to work while other people are playing and delay thoughts of gratification until your new venture is all the way up and running. While this is easy to say, many people find it much more difficult to commit to in practice. As such, you will find that you are more successful at it when it counts if you don't wait until the rubber hits the road to start practicing. Live every day in a self-disciplined manner and you will find it much easier to keep up the good work when it matters most.

Keep your goals in mind: If you hope to find success in just 18-months then you are going to need to remain focused on that fact every hour of every day. When the going gets tough, let your dedication to your goal be enough to keep you motivated and keep you moving forward. When things fall apart due to unforeseen circumstances, don't focus on the negatives and instead just keep moving forward. As long as you keep your goal in mind you will find that everything else that gets in your way is little more than an easily avoidable distraction between you and true success.

Don't be afraid of hard work: The average millionaire works sixty hours per week. In order to meet your goal in the next 18-months you are likely going to need to spend forty hours per week working to survive and nearly that many preparing your investment strategy, hiring a team, finding a way to pay for it, finding properties and ensuring they are ready to be sold or rented when the time comes. Don't waste your work time, make every hour count.

Follow through on your plan: This book outlines the steps you need to take in order to ensure you make $100,000 per year in real estate investing starting with an 18-month period of preparation. In order to do so you are going to need to prioritize the activities in the right way and focus on completing them in the correct order to maximize your effectiveness. Each day you should make a point of considering what the best use of your time is at any given point and then doing everything you can to follow through on that action.

Never stop learning: There are always new and improved ways for finding new properties and maximizing the value of the properties that you do own coming into existence. Resting on your laurels, even after the first 18 months is only going to lead to decreasing returns over time. Even once you hit your goal, you can still do better, make it a point of studying real estate for at least an hour per day while you are getting started, and then at least an hour per week when you are on your way. Listen to podcasts about it, read books, take classes and seminars, immersing yourself in the topic will only lead to greater success in the long run.

Remove failure from your vocabulary: Seventy percent of people who attempt to invest in real estate in the way you are attempting to fail to achieve their goals for one reason or another. This doesn't matter however, because you aren't going to be one of them. Strive to develop a positive mindset and don't let anything get between you and your belief in success. Failing and persevering will only make you stronger, it is the fear of failure that is likely to hold you back. Take calculated risks towards achieving your goals and never be afraid of following through on them just because success is not guaranteed.

Look for the right opportunities: Those with a successful real estate investment mindset don't approach opportunities by thinking about what it will cost them, they consider what the opportunity could net them assuming it works out correctly. Thinking about things in terms of cost helps to create a limiting mindset, thinking about them in terms of the value they provide will allow you focus your time, energy and money towards the things that will do the most good the greatest percentage of the time.

If the benefits are worth the price, then you should be willing to go for it, no matter what that price is. There is always a way to find the money for a profitable venture, regardless of whether you have it in your pocket right now. It is important to not let a lack of immediate funds slow you down when it comes to hitting your goals. Instead of focusing on what you don't have, spend that energy considering the various ways you can crunch the numbers, work the system and take as full advantage of the opportunity as you possibly can.

Chapter 2: Finding the Money

One of the many difficult things about getting started in real estate, assuming you don't have $100,000 plus sitting around, is finding the right way to pay for your initial investment in a way that makes the most sense for you. Luckily, there are numerous different options to choose from in order to get someone else to bear the brunt of the upfront costs. Before you start looking in earnest, however, it is crucial that you do some homework up front in order to know exactly what you are getting into.

Borrowing from a position of strength

In order to ensure you get the best deal on your loan as possible, it is important to know what tools you have at your disposal when it comes to finding the right type of financing. To get started, you are going to want to check your credit report and seek professional help if your score isn't where you want it to be. Unfortunately, a high credit score isn't all that is required these days as the Great Recession has made it much more difficult to finance an investment property than it once was. This means you will naturally start at a disadvantage if you don't have an extensive credit history or lots of previous investment experience. Difficult is a long way from impossible, however, as long as you approach lenders with the following:

Significant down payment: Currently most traditional lenders are going to require that you have at least 20 percent of the total cost of the investment you are requesting financing for in hand before they will give the go ahead. If you are considering hard money lenders (discussed in detail later in this chapter) then you will likely need 40 percent instead. However, if you can put down an extra 5 percent then you will likely start to see a significant decrease in rates almost immediately. Being able to offer up a larger down payment will also make it more likely that financial institutions will be more forgiving when it comes to overlooking less than perfect credit; this will only take you so far, however.

If you don't have the full 20 percent down payment for the property you are considering, but you qualify for a bank loan in all other respects, then you may want to consider getting two loans rather than just one, just keep in mind that it is going to cut into your profits substantially and it can be more difficult than getting just one mortgage as well. If you do pursue this course of action, however, it is important that you strive to pay off one of the mortgages as quickly as possible to cut down on the interest you will pay.

Have the right credit rating: Once you know your credit rating you will be able to more readily determine what type of loan you can expect to find and what the interest rates are likely to be. Anything that is below 740 is going to cost you in terms of interest rates and monthly payments and interest rate hikes. In general, this typically works out to about 2 additional points of interest for every 10 points your credit score drops. If you are looking for a lower payment amount then you will have a higher amount of interest and vice versa.

Furthermore, prior to going to see any lenders you are going to want to gather up a list of all of your investment and personal expenses for the previous six months along with proof that you can afford them plus the additional expenses that the loan will add to your plate.

Ask the right lenders: If you don't meet, or even better exceed, the minimum requirements for the larger financial institutions then you will likely be better off looking into alternatives rather than taking the less favorable loan these lenders will give. The best place to start is going to be local credit unions as their requirements are typically laxer than the major players, especially if your property is in their area. These lenders often have a strong interest in seeing their local area prosper which means they will be more likely to look the other way on things that would be deal breakers with larger lenders.

Another viable choice these days is to ask for owner financing. Prior to the Great Recession, when virtually anyone with a pulse could get a bank loan, asking for owner financing was a turnoff to potential sellers because it meant your credit was absolutely in the pits. This perception has changed, however, and now approximately 20 percent of all sellers are willing to consider the idea at the very least. If you do obtain owner financing you will then sign a promissory note that outlines the specifics of the agreement including how long it will take you to pay back the loan and what the interest rate is going to be.

Other lender options

Long-term considerations: As you are not looking to purchase just one investment properly, but looking to make this a regular occurrence, you are going to want to put in the time upfront to find a lender that you are comfortable building a long-term relationship with. While it will require extra work up front, this relationship will ultimately make it easier to complete the loan process in the future. You will be able to work together to form a strategy that will help to ensure that everyone comes out on top in the long run. You will want to be wary of taking a loan from a real estate broker, however, as they are going to be much pickier about the types of properties you are free to purchase.

You will also need to keep in mind that the lender is going to directly distributing your loans which means you are going to want to interview them before you sign anything. You should always ask every lender the following questions:
- How many investors total are you currently working with?
- What is the maximum number of loans you allow individual investors to have active at a single time?

- Are there some types of real estate investments you typically favor over others?

These questions will then make it easier for you to confidently choose the right lender for you based not on a sales pitch but on cold hard facts. It will also allow you to alter your pitch based on what you've learned, if appropriate. If you don't like the answers you receive, you will then be able to move on and keep from wasting your time either waiting to be preapproved for a loan or from being given rates that you aren't going to be able to profit from.

Hard money loans: If you are looking for an alternative to traditional lenders, or simply don't have the credit to qualify for one of their loans, then a hard money loan might be a good choice. A hard money loan is a loan that is provided by a private investor instead of a bank or a credit union. These loans will generally be for shorter periods of time and the majority of the payments you will make will go towards interest with a large balloon payment coming at the end of the cycle to square up on the principal of the loan.

Hard money loans are frequently appealing to new real estate investors due to the fact that the lender is going to be more interested in the quality of the proffered investment opportunity than if you have successfully invested in real estate before. When it comes to determining the right hard money lender to use, the best place to start looking is at your local real estate investment club. In general, when it comes to finding out details on investment in your area, then a real estate investment club is a great place to start as you will almost always find someone who can show you the ropes.

Finding a local club should be as easy as getting online and doing a little research and even mid-sized towns are likely to have one or two meeting somewhere on a regular basis. Even if you don't end up getting a loan through the connections you make there it will still likely pay off in one way or another down the line as there are plenty of things these folks can teach you.

When looking into different hard money lenders you are going to want to keep in mind that they typically focus on different types of real estate deals. Most hard money lenders operate via what is known as first lien position. This means they are going to be the first ones to get their money back if you end up selling the property off early due to unforeseen circumstances. Second lien position hard money lenders, those who would get their money back after your initial investment was recouped, can be found, though they are much rarer.

The interest rates you will be able to find when it comes to hard money loans are generally going to vary based on your location as well as the number of other hard money lenders in the area. In general, however, the amount is always going to be higher than what a bank is going to charge and will typically be in the 10 to 15 percent range with the specifics of your investment and your personal finances going a long way to move the average a few points one way or another. Additionally, points will range between 2 and 4 percent on the amount of the loan.

The total amount that a hard money lender will be willing to put forth will be based on what is known as the loan to value ratio. This ratio can be found by taking the value of the potential loan and then dividing that number by the total value of the loan and dividing it by the total estimated value of the property you are trying to purchase once it has been completely renovated. In general, a hard money lender will be willing to give you anywhere from 65 to 75 percent of the value of the property in question.

It is also possible to find hard money lenders who will pay almost the full amount required or even chip in for the costs of the renovations. These are a much riskier proposition though which means they will expect as much as 20 percent of the total profits when things are said and done. If you are looking to get started with little or no money down then it can be worth the decrease in overall profit.

When approaching a hard money lender, you are going to be sure that you really have all your ducks in a row in order to do your best to guarantee your success. As such, you will want to have a credit score that is at least 600 along with an income debt ratio below 45 percent and a credit history that has been clean from foreclosures or bankruptcies for at least 10 years. You will also need to show that you can afford all of your expenses plus the payments that would be required. Finally, you will need to show that you will have equity invested in the property that will function as collateral to ensure you will pay back the loan as opposed to vanishing into the night.

Alternately, you may want to consider alternatives to investment loans, especially if you are looking to put down as little as possible up front. Title loans, equity loans based on other property you own or even credit cards can all help you to get started though they should only be used as a last resort because the rates and payments are always going to be much higher than even slightly more conventional options.

Chapter 3: Mistakes to Avoid

As a new investor in the real estate market, you will likely find that every move you consider making fills you with anxiety, simply each and every action has the potential to affect you so greatly for good or for ill. This is a natural part of the learning process, however, and learning while doing is naturally going to lead to some mistakes now and then. While you will want to view any potential mistakes as learning experiences, there are some that you definitely don't want to experience for yourself. Keep the following in mind and avoid these major new investor pitfalls at all costs.

Planning at the viewing: If you find yourself looking at a potential property without first having a clear plan for utilizing it effectively already in mind then you are already starting off at a huge disadvantage when it comes to deciding the right amount to offer for the property. If you don't already know everything about the property beforehand then it will be much more difficult to make an offer that is sure to make you as much money as possible from it. When working towards your 18-month plan, you are going to have very little wiggle room when it comes to getting everything just right, which means knowing your numbers is a must if you want to stay on track.

Many new investors fall into the business by initially purchasing a property for a price that they feel is simply too good to pass up.

They then find themselves with property in hand and no real clue as to how they are going to move forward. The reality of the matter is that if you haven't even done research on the local market then you won't actually know if the price you paid was a steal or if you were taken advantage of. When considering property investments, it is always important to remember that just because a given property is a good deal, doesn't mean it is a good deal for you, right now. With early real estate investment deals you have too much on the line to do yourself the disservice of moving forward with a property before having an airtight course of action ready to go. Pricing out properties is discussed in more detail in chapters 5 and 6.

Not keeping your expectations in check: While some properties can quickly and easily be turned around for a substantial profit, these are the exception, not the rule. In order to meet the strict 18-month deadline, you are going to need to start with properties that need a lot of work, which means having a realistic timeframe for just how long everything is going to take, and thus when you can expect to see a profit, is crucial when it comes to ensuring that you will be prepared both mentally and financially for the tribulations to come. To understand the average timeframe, consider the following regarding just what a successful real estate investment entails.

First you will need to do the research on the area you are considering investing in as well as researching numerous different options before finding one that meets your needs. Then, once you make an offer, you can expect to wait for upwards of three months if you have gone ahead and gotten preapproval through a traditional bank. Even if everything is aces, you will still likely need to factor in about a month before your name is on the deed.

Selling a property can be a process that moves quickly from the very first open house. Unfortunately, it can also drag on insufferably, largely based on factors that are outside of your control. While the stars can align and random chance can work in your favor, the odds that somewhere along the process something is going to go wrong are too high not to factor into the process. Speed is not one of real estate's investing's virtues but what it lacks in quick turnaround times it makes up for in reliability.

Thinking you can do it all yourself: While having faith in yourself is an admirable quality, when it comes to real estate investment odds are not only will you not be able to do it all yourself, you are almost certainly not going to want to, especially if you want to hit that 18-month window. While some people will have all the skills required to complete a house full of renovations all by themselves, the time that this will take will almost always mean that this is a poor value proposition at best. You are going to want to complete between two and three complete flips in an 18-month window and that is not something anyone can realistically expect to do on their own.

Real estate investment is a numbers game which means that you will always see greater overall returns by taking a smaller personal cut of each property and working quickly and efficiently with a team than trying to make as much profit as possible and doing it all yourself. At the very least, you are going to need a real estate investment lawyer, a CPA and a reliable contractor. The specifics on building a team are discussed in the next chapter.

The importance of nurturing these relationships once you have them cannot be over-stressed. They will quite often be the difference between success and failure. You will be working with these individuals on a regular basis and you will need their help to generate the type of active or passive income stream that you are looking for. Go out of you want to build trust and form bonds beyond the realm of the traditional service person/customer relationship. While the extra work might seem pointless at first, the results will more than pay for themselves with time.

Never getting the best deals possible: While you won't be able to take every negotiation to the point where you are getting your ideal price every single time, it is important to not let things get to the point where you are routinely giving up more than you should just to close a deal. These concessions, while seemingly minor, can easily add up over time, pushing your goal of $100,000 per year back in the process. When going into every negotiation, you are going to need to know what your ideal number is going to be, the maximum amount you can give up and still make the minimum profit you need to move forward with the project and the number where you are simply going to want to walk away because the deal is no longer profitable.

Additionally, you are going to want to stick to this philosophy regardless if you are putting down money on a new property or simply buying a box of nails from the hardware store. While these smaller numbers might not seem like much individually, they too will add up overtime and account for a significant drain on your profits if left unchecked. Be sure not to let a lax attitude affect your bottom line, always be aware of the true cost of any concessions you make.

Not knowing what you're signing: Another problem that many new real estate investors run into is after they go to the trouble of doing their research, make a plan based around a specific property, then then rush through the loan acquisition process without making sure they understand the finer points of the contract they end up signing. Not having a clear understanding of these finer points is akin to gambling with your long-term investment, a poor choice no matter what situation you find yourself in. Failing to understand the specifics of your loan agreement can easily lead you to paying thousands more than you were anticipating based on inaccurate assumptions alone.

Lowballing renovation costs: Early on you may find that it is difficult for you to accurately determine the cost for the specific renovations a property might need as you have never had to do so before. Underestimating these costs can be dangerous, however, as it can end up leaving you in a position where you have committed all your available resources to a project and still come up short. This is why you will always be better off overestimating these costs while also factoring in the maintenance fees that will be required while you are trying to get the property sold. Don't forget the insurance and taxes as well. Over time, when working with a contractor, you should get a feel for what these sorts of things typically cost.

Treating investments casually: Just because investing in real estate is often thought of as a long-term investment doesn't mean that you can afford to approach it casually, especially if you hope to start seeing serious results in just 18 months. Your real estate investments are a business and should be treated as such. Only by showing real dedication and true commitment will you ever realistically see a reliable return; when it comes to investments you will only ever get back from them what you put in multiplied by the amount of effort you put forth.

Chapter 4: Getting Started with Your 18-month Strategy

The basic outline of the 18-month strategy to help you to earn $100,000 per year revolves around finding ugly duckling properties, polishing them until they shine and then selling them for a significant profit. If you can do this just three or four times over the course of the first 18 months then you will have netted your first $100,000 and be on your way to setting up a system whereby you can safely assume the money will keep rolling in. Once you reach that point. you will then want to slowly start shifting from fixing and flipping properties to fixing and holding them to rent out in order to ensure a passive income stream that will last you for the rest of your life. The details for doing both can be found in the next two chapters.

Ugly duckling properties: An ugly duckling property is simply a property that most people would not think of looking at twice simply because it needs a bit of extra work. The more extra work required, the greater the potential for profit once you have fixed it up and found its inner beauty.

While the potential for profit with ugly duckling properties is going to be higher than with properties that are more or less ready to resell right away, the risk is also going to be higher as well. Ugly duckling properties can have any number of unexpected surprises attached which can turn an otherwise stellar investment into an unmitigated nightmare. This means you are always going to want to have a backup plan in case the original plan for the property doesn't pan out like you hoped. At the very least, you need to consider that the property may very will sit unsold and vacant for a prolonged period of time.

Investing in ugly duckling properties, and thus following this 18-month plan, isn't going to be right for everyone. It has proven to be the correct investment choice for those who like to be directly in charge of their own investments, like the idea of being able to hold their investments in their hands, and even walk around inside them, and enjoy finding a great deal even if it takes a little extra work.

The key to finding good ugly duckling properties is the ability to see past whatever it is that is causing the property in question to be seen as an ugly duckling and see the potential for risk and reward instead. This means you will need to be able to determine what the likely renovation costs are going to be, or pay someone to do it for you, and then determine if the overall potential for profit is going to be worth the price of admission.

Finding the right properties
In order to take your first steps to making the 18-month plan a reality, the first thing you are going to need to do is to find the right properties. To find the types of properties you are looking

for, you are going to want to forgo the typical channels and go where the real potential for profit lives.

Motivated sellers: One of the best ways to find property that lots of investors aren't already fighting over is to find sellers before they make it into the system. Once a seller has a real estate agent, the odds of getting the best possible price decreases dramatically. This means you are going to want to reach out to sellers before they realize they want to sell. The best candidate for this process is what is known as a motivated seller. These are individuals who have pressing financial needs that need to be cleared up ASAP. You then have the ability to step in with an offer that can make the issue go away and everyone (but mostly you) wins.

While it may sound surprising, the best way to find motivated sellers is through a direct marketing campaign. Assuming you live in at least a city of a medium size, you should be able to find a local company that will sell you a list of people who are currently sitting on a sizeable pile of debt for a few hundred dollars. With these details in hand, you simply do a little digging at the County Clerk's office and cross off everyone who doesn't currently own their home.

Once you have a list of potential sellers you then simply draft a form letter outlining the fact that you have found out (don't say how) that they are in financial trouble and explain that you are offering a solution, in cash. Make sure to express regret at their hardship as well and indicate that you are on their side. You don't want to make an offer in the letter, however, but instead express interest in getting together and discussing the situation in detail.

While every letter won't lead to success, out of about 300 possible hits you will likely come back with around 10 individuals who are interested in what you have to say which should be enough to get you started. From there it is simply a matter of assessing the value of the property compared to what the individual owes and then lowballing them enough to ensure that you can still make a sizeable profit even after repairs and renovations have been completed.

Find a team
Regardless of how handy you feel you are, it is virtually impossible to make it through an entire renovation by yourself, especially in a timeframe that will gel with the 18-month plan. As such, it is important to go out of your way to establish a strong team to help you out early on, as doing so will pay dividends for years to come, even after the costs of using them are taken into account.

The first person you are going to want to hire is a real estate lawyer and a certified public accountant that specializes in handling real estate investments. While you will hopefully never have to make serious use of these individuals, having them in your pocket will make any situations where you do imminently more manageable. These services are going to be costly, though the fees are not regulated which means you will be able to shop around or negotiate a price, just be sure not to sacrifice quality in service of saving a few dollars.

Next you will want to find a good real estate agent who will be able to help you sell the properties as quickly as possible once they are ready to go. While you can skip this recommendation, and set up your own open houses and advertising, your goal should be to turn around the property as quickly as possible and a good real estate agent will be worth their commission if they can do this reliably. They will also have access to channels that you don't and will sometimes be able to help you find properties as well. A good working relationship with a real estate agent can truly help you take your real estate investing to the next level.

General contractor: A reliable general contractor is worth their weight in gold. This person will be in charge of the day to day work on your investment property and will ideally come with their own crew as well which means you won't need to go out of you way to hire a dozen different specialists. While finding the right contractor can be time consuming, it will be time well spent if you follow through on it properly. The best way to find a good contractor is to start by getting recommendations, ideally from a local real estate investment club or from someone else who has reason to know what they are talking about. Barring that, you can visit local lumber mills and ask them for the names of the contractors who always use the highest quality materials as that is typically a sign of good work all-around.

You will then want to take your list and meet with the contractors face to face. In person interviews are crucial as you will, in theory, be working with one of these individuals on a regular basis which means it is important that you get along on a personal as well as a professional level. During the interviews, you are going to want to find out what types of projects they are comfortable handling, references, what type of team they bring to the table and the number of jobs they typically take on at once. Ideally you will want to end up with a primary contractor and a backup contractor to ensure you can start any new job before the ink has fully dried on the contract.

Chapter 5: Flipping Properties

Flipping ugly duckling properties is the key to making $100,000 in 18-months and then using those profits to generate a steady return of $100,000 per year from your investments. In order to do so reliably you are going to want to have a team in place and already have done the required research when it comes to finding good deals.

Fundamentals

ARV: The most important number when it comes to any potential property is the After Repair Value (ARV). ARV is the amount you will be able to plan on selling the home for one everything about it has been improved to the point of show condition. You will always want to underestimate the ARV due to the fact that overestimation can easily lead to a significant decrease in the profits you make once everything is said and done.

In order to determine the ARV, you are going to want to take the amount you can get the property for and add to it the amount it will cost to fix it up along with any fees you may be paying for use of the money you are using to do so. The end result should be less than 70 percent of what you plan to make on the property and that number should equal between $25,000 and $30,000 depending on the amount of work that needs to be done to the property as you will need to do between three and four successful flips to hit your goal. If the property doesn't hit these numbers then you will want to move on as there are better choices out there.

It is important to have a clear understanding of what the ARV is likely to be when you go an visit the property for the first time as this will ensure that you won't have to worry about your emotions getting in the way of making the right decision or having to determine the ARV after the fact. While sticking to this rule might seem unnecessarily strict, shifting even 5 percent away from it can lead to significant losses, especially if issues arise that you didn't foresee.

Understand the likely buyers: When it comes to setting the right ARV, it is important to also understand who you are going to be targeting as your buyers when everything is said and done. This will ensure you can accurately determine the quality of the overall remodel as well as what you will be able to sell the property for. If you are looking at properties in rural areas then you will want to ensure there is plenty of room for animals and ancillary vehicles, as well as fewer government restrictions. On the other hand, areas with good school and family-friendly amenities are going to attract families which means you are going to want to prioritize yard space and extra bathrooms.

There is money to be made from all different types of properties, regardless of the layout, as long as you have a clear idea of who you are creating the home for. Play to the strengths of the property and you will not only save on remodeling costs, you will find that selling the property is easier in the long run as well.

Understand the value you create: As you make improvements to a property, it is important to keep a running tally of the value you are adding to it. Likewise, it is important to take plenty of before pictures to show to potential buyers so they can see how much the property has improved which helps to justify your asking price. This is not to say that you need to completely gut every property completely and more or less start from scratch, it is important to never begin an improvement if it is going to cost more than the amount of value it adds to the final selling price.

While you aren't going to want to leave things in a faulty or unsafe condition, you are also going to want to think twice before doing things like renovating a living room that is a little smaller than average. Your bottom line should always be in the front of your mind when you are making a list of changes your team needs to implement.

When it comes to things such as decorating and painting, you are always going to want to stick with neutral colors, not plain white, and go with generic decisions whenever possible. Whatever you do, you want it to be as easy as possible for a wide variety of people to be able to move in and transplant their style with ease. Everyone who sees the completed property should be able to immediately see themselves living there and an aggressive color or style choice is only going to appeal to a limited portion of the population.

Two things that you are always going to want to update are going to be the fixtures in the kitchen and those in the bathroom. A small change in these spaces can go a long way towards making older homes feel fresh while only adding a small cost to your bottom line. This includes things like light switch covers, mirrors and faucets. While a new toilet and shower can quickly send costs spiraling to epic heights, a $120 sink can easily change the entire feel of a bathroom.

In the kitchen, you are also always going to want to modernize the cabinet doors as this will change the feel of the whole space dramatically. If they are in good working order, the refrigerator and the oven can be left as they are, as long as they are clean enough to be mistaken as new. Skipping this step can leave a perceived layer of grime throughout the space that hurts your sale's chances time and again. As such, you should always hire a professional cleaning service prior to showing the house no matter what.

Don't get too attached: While it is important to do everything in your power in order to ensure that a property is going to look as good as possible, at the same time you are going to want to everything in your power to ensure that you remain relatively divorced from the proceedings so you can keep a critical eye on things as they progress. If you aren't careful, it is very easy to find yourself growing attached to the property and letting your emotions influence the price you think it is worth. This is always going to be a folly however, as the only things that should alter the ARV of the property once you have purchased it are the market value in the area and the strength of the market overall. Don't forget, you shouldn't be striving for the maximum price possible, you should be prioritizing speed of sale. The faster you manage to sell the property, the faster you will be able to get down to getting business finding another to repeat the process with.

Keeping costs down

Break tasks down to component parts: While staring at everything that needs to be done to a property is enough to give most people a panic attack, it helps to break tasks down into their component parts. Not only will this make it easier to cope with what needs to be accomplished, you will also save money because you will be able to determine what is required for each job up front which means you are more likely to get a bulk discount. You will want to go room by room and make a list of what needs to be done so you can be sure you don't miss anything, and also show that list to potential buyers when the time comes to sell.

Nurture supplier relationships: When you are first getting started flipping properties you are going to want to do additional legwork up front so that you can count on getting better prices in the long-term on products you know you are going to be buying in bulk time and again. Keep in mind that running to the store and buying parts last minute is going to be a serious drain on your profits if it is not kept in check.

Instead, purchasing products in bulk from a local supplier will not only allow you to establish the price for things more accurately at the start, it will lead to additional savings if done appropriately. To get started, all you need to do is ask to speak to the manager at the local hardware or construction supply store. The best bet in these cases is to find a local business instead of a chain as they will likely be more willing and able to make a deal.

After you find the right person to talk to, you will want to show them your list of products and let them know that you are going to be in the renovation business for a long time and that you are looking to establish mutually beneficial relationships now, to save yourself time later. Once it is clear what you are offering, all you need to do is to ask what type of discount they might be able to provide on your bulk orders in exchange for assurances that you will be doing all of your business at their store for the foreseeable future. While this won't work every time, it shouldn't take you more than a few stops to find someone who is willing to make a deal.

Always be on the lookout for deals: In addition to buying in bulk, you are going to want to get into the habit of keeping an eye out for good deals on products that could be potentially useful in future renovations and stock up while the price is right. One particular area that it is frequently worth keeping an eye out for deals is when it comes to granite for smaller countertops. A granite countertop will add a good deal of class to a master bathroom, but the costs on fresh granite can be quite steep. As such, you can keep an eye out for pieces of granite that have major flaws in the middle, and then have your team cut them yourselves and pick them up for sometimes as much as 20 percent of the regular price.

Chapter 6: Rental Properties

Once you have successfully made your first $100,000, you will want to start looking at relevant properties with a different eye. While you will want to ensure that you are flipping enough houses to ensure that your extra income remains stable, you will also want to start picking properties to hold on to. Rental properties are a great long-term investment strategy that can generate a significant amount of monthly revenue, especially if you pick them up on the cheap as ugly-duckling properties to start with, and have most, if not all, of the asking price ready to go up front.

Rental renovation tips
While most of what passed for reliable advice in the previous chapter will still apply, there are a few additional factors you are going to want to keep in mind when it comes to renovating properties for rent as opposed to sale.

Cut costs in the right places: While it will still be extremely important to do all that you can in order to get rid of the ugly duckling vibe from the property in order to promote rentability, renters aren't buyers which means that you don't need to do as much to ensure the property is perfect. A good rule of thumb with rental properties is that you are going to want to focus on the areas that will make the property easier to rent out. This means you are going to want to stick to basic livability changes in the bedrooms and then focus on the bathrooms and kitchen, including fixtures, countertops and cabinets which means you can typically do both rooms for about $1,000 total.

Look for good prices, not cheap materials: While you might be tempted to go with the cheapest options available when it comes to rental properties, you need to make sure that you aren't going to end up actually costing yourself more in the long run. Cheaper products tend to wear out more quickly, typically twice as fast, than products that are as little as 20 percent more expensive which means you are going to have to replace them year after year. It is typically better to get the majority of your costs out of the way upfront as opposed to replacing cheap products on a regular basis.

Rental property math

Property management: If you are interested in managing the property yourself, you are likely going to be in a better position to do so than most, simply because you already have a contractor you can call when it comes to doing repairs on the property and a list of suppliers who can give you a good deal on parts. However, if you are interested in generating passive income from your rental properties then you will want to look into a property management company. Property management companies will deal with tenants directly so you don't have to, which is a big plus for many landlords.

When it comes to using property management companies, it is important to do your research regarding which one makes the most since for you. The average cost of one of these companies is between 8 and 12 percent of the monthly rental price. When you are first starting out you will likely need to add as much as an extra 10 percent on top of this costs as very few property management companies are going to be interested in working with a single, single family home. While these fees will eventually drop as you find more properties to rent out, this is likely what you can expect to pay from the start.

Pricing your rental: You should already have a general idea of what you are planning to charge for the property based on the ARV and the rates of similar rental properties in the area. From there you will want to consider any marketable extras you have added to the property as well as anything about it that makes it unique for the market. The goal here should be to ensure you aren't shortchanging yourself while also not overestimating the work that has been done, remember, the more expensive the property the greater the likelihood that it is going to sit empty prior to finding a renter.

If you are having trouble determining what to charge for the property, you will want to first consider what tier the property falls into now that it has been fixed up. The highest tier of property is going to be those that are likely going to attract the best tenants possible and it is unlikely you will ever have trouble finding tenants who will pay top dollar for the privilege of living there. Very few ugly duckling properties are going to reach this tier. Second tier properties are the most common types of rentals that you see, they are not the pick of the litter but they are well-constructed homes in average or better neighborhoods, not flashy but not shabby either. When fixing up an ugly duckling property you will want to shoot for this tier.

For tier two properties the overall risk of vacancy is still going to be relatively low, and if there is a vacancy it is unlikely to last more than a month. As you likely got the property for a great deal, you are going to want to strive to get back 2 percent of your total investment per month in rent which means the property will be purely making money in just about five years. As such, if you paid $100,000 for the property and the renovations then you would want to charge $2,000 per month to see a reasonable return on your investment eventually.

If you end up with a third-tier property, either because the renovations didn't work out as smoothly as you hoped or if the neighbor is on the rougher side then you are going to need to charge more for rent to balance out the additional risks associated with the investment. These properties will likely sit empty for two months or more between tenants and you will want to be less strict when it comes to choosing tenants as they are unlikely to stick around for more than the length of their lease anyway. You will want to aim for 3 percent of your investment per month with these properties for the best results.

In addition to what you will be making in rent, when it comes to determining what your long-term profits will be you are going to need to factor in the average 3 percent that most properties appreciate by per year. Unfortunately, you are also going to need to subtract out fees associated with maintenance costs, property management fees, repairs, taxes, insurance and months where the property sits vacant. Furthermore, you may find it a helpful exercise to assume that a full 50 percent of your yearly profits are going to be squandered by major repairs or by responding to other types of emergencies. While this won't always be the case, when the repairs are required they are likely to be quite expensive so it should all balance out in the end.

While this might not leave much coming in as pure profit per month, you will need to think about the property in terms of its long-term value instead. You never know when the market is going to experience a huge jump in your favor and it will suddenly make more sense to sell off the property and take advantage of the market scarcity to make a huge profit. Regardless, you are likely going to be seeing greater than the average 7 return on investment that many investments see, and the volatility for housing investments is practically non-existent. With enough investment properties, you won't even need to complete fix and flips anymore.

Advertising

Once you are ready to rent out a property it is important to do everything you can to ensure the vacancy is filled as quickly as possible. The day after renovations are completed is the day the property starts costing you money while it is sitting vacant. When it comes to getting the most effective advertising for a new rental property for the cheapest price, the best place to start is with social media.

You are going to want to start the social media campaign for the property on the day that you start the renovations. Taking pictures of the property throughout the process will serve as a timeline showing how much value has been added to it through the work you have done. Having digital proof of these things will help to ease the minds of potential renters as they won't simply have to take your word that specific repairs were done.

What's more, studies show that each person is never more than three degrees of separation from someone that is in the market for a new place to live at least 50 percent of the time which means that making sure your property gets in front of as many eyes as possible is a great way to find prospective tenants. If you can spread the word to just twenty people outside of your personal social circle then you are quite likely to find a renter without even having to worry about posting a for rent sign in the front yard.

Screening tenants

Once you have found some prospective tenants, the next thing you will need to do is find the most reliable one to start paying you rent without destroying all the value you have already added to the property. The first thing you are going to need to do to get this process underway is understand the landlord laws in your area to make sure that you are exercising your rights as fully as possible while at the same time not infringing on the rights of your future tenants.

The screening policy that is right for you is going to be as unique as your overall investment plan, simply because different things are going to be right for different landlords. Some will feel the need to exacting in their tenant selection process and others will feel comfortable knowing just the basics of who they are renting to. While the right approach for you is likely somewhere in the middle of these extremes, what a lot of it is going to come down to is what level of risk you feel is acceptable. If you are too strict then you run the risk of turning away potentially viable tenants and if you are too lenient then you run the risk of losing value on your property. Regardless of where you fall on the spectrum, you are going to want to keep a few crucial considerations in mind.

First and foremost, you are going to want to ensure that they haven't had any evictions within the last ten years. While a lot can happen in ten years and going back to far can punish responsible adults for youthful transactions, this is enough time to protect you from serial renters who move from place to place, staying only long enough to be evicted. For your first rental property a firm stance of no evictions, period, is perfectly acceptable.

You will also want to look at references from employers and previous landlords, even if you don't use them. Having tenants who are confident enough to put down this information is typically a strong enough sign that they expect the results to be positive. If you do follow up, as a potential landlord you have the right to ask basic relevant questions, just be sure not to pry unduly.

A background check should be a non-negotiable part of your screening process. Felonies that include violent crimes and dangerous drugs should be enough to disqualify potential tenants under most circumstances, though you may want to give the felon the chance to explain what happened. Keeping things simple and avoiding anyone with a felony in the past 10 years is often enough to weed out the riff-raff.

When it comes to determining the right level of income for your new tenant(s), it is important to ensure that they are always going to be able to pay the rent no matter what. As such, an income total of all relevant parties that is at least three times the total of the rent should be enough to prevent you from holding the bag should times get tough.

If your screening turns up things that you like, it is important to always send out a rejection letter to the would-be tenant. This is known as an adverse actions letter and it will let them know what actions you took as part of the screening process, what the results you revealed and why you made the decision you did. You will need to send this out within sixty days of when the screening was completed to comply with federal law.

Conclusion

Thank you for making it through to the end of *Property Investing: How to Create Wealth and Passive Income Through Smart Buy & Hold Real Estate Investing. An Exact 18-Month Strategy for Making an Extra 100k Per Year*, let's hope it was informative and able to provide you with all of the tools you need to achieve your goals in just 18 months.

The next step is to stop reading about real estate investment and to get your boots on the ground and start making it a reality for you. The only way to be successful with this plan is to dedicate the next year and a half to it, come hell or high water. Remember, while it may seem as though the odds are stacked against you, as long as you persevere you really can make your dreams a reality.

Finally, if you found this book useful in anyway, a review on Amazon is always appreciated!

Description

If you are interested in leaving the 9-to-5 world behind and instead being your own boss while still making six figures per year, then *Property Investing: How to Create Wealth and Passive Income Through Smart Buy & Hold Real Estate Investing. An Exact 18-Month Strategy for Making an Extra 100k Per Year* is the book you have been waiting for.

Real estate investment is one of the oldest and most reliable forms of investment in the world and if you follow the plan outlined inside you can start seeing real results in just a year and a half. While it might sound too good to be true, this is no get rich quick scheme, it is simply an accelerated way of taking advantage of the real estate market, the same way that Warren Buffet, Donald Trump and countless others have done for generations. All it takes is hard work, determination, and a little luck, and before you know it you will not only be generating a six-figure income, you will be on your way to building long-term passive income as well.

So, what are you waiting for? Stop waiting for your ship to come in and grab the bull by the horns. Take control of your financial future and buy this book today!

Inside you will find

- How to train your brain to be ready for true financial success through a property investment mindset.
- Surefire ways of funding your first real estate investment with as little as no money down.
- The easiest way of finding sellers who are just waiting for you to take their home off their hands.
- One simple trick for ensuring that you never overpay for a property investment.
- The easiest way to find rental properties that are sure to turn a profit
- *And more...*

www.ingramcontent.com/pod-product-compliance
Lightning Source LLC
Chambersburg PA
CBHW050027230526
45470CB00003B/1167